A JOURNEY TO WHOLENESS

Copyright © 2024 by Danae Beckford

All rights reserved. No part of this book may be reproduced in any manner whatsoever without written permission except in the case of brief quotations embodied in critical articles and reviews.

First Printing, 2024

A Journey To Wholeness

IDENTITY, AUTHENTIC LIVING, AND BEING IN ALIGNMENT WITH THE SPIRIT

Danae Beckford

Danae Beckford

Contents

Dedication		ix
1	Acknowledge	1
2	Dream	16
3	Give	50
4	Expect	57
5	Grow	66
6	Shift	82
7	Manifest	95
8	Be present	109
9	Realize	121
10	Choose	129
11	Honor	182
12	Allow	188
13	Purpose	204
14	Rest	220
15	Identity	233

16	I am	280
17	Peace	306
18	Love	340
19	Joy	357
20	Happiness	379
21	Action	389

For Elaine and Karen
When two worlds collide

1

Acknowledge

I see you.

To acknowledge is to say, "I see you."

What do you see? What have you acknowledged? What do you understand? Have you accepted, or are you hiding?

I think it is important to understand whether or not we acknowledge something. Whatever it is, this thing has power. All power is given to it by means of self. Living with its presence daily, whether or not we choose to engage with it.

When we choose to acknowledge, we take on the role of self-empowerment. We begin to utilize the presence of fear, anger, guilt, joy, laughter, rage, sadness, annoyance, boredom, anxiety, confidence, and many others to propel ourselves forward into a realm of conscious living.

To acknowledge is to say that you will no longer allow life to happen to you, but rather you will use the energy around you to curate the life you want to unfold.

Without acknowledgement, we become "victims" to our circumstances. We become disempowered and begin feeling like there is nothing we can do to change the narrative of our lives. We believe that we cannot, so we do not. We think our existence is not enough, so we do not occupy and create space for ourselves. We do not acknowledge the role we play in our stagnancy. Everything is happening to us, yet we do nothing but allow it.

To acknowledge is to realize the power of self. It is to open our eyes to the creative force that each and every one of us carries inside. To acknowledge is to see self and move freely in our being. It is allowing the freedom of self to no longer be held captive to people, places, or things.

Acknowledging is literally choosing to escape the captivity of your mind and thrusting yourself into the world of the unknown. To acknowledge is to take a quantum leap into an abyss and allow yourself to learn as you go.

Ultimately, to acknowledge is to choose to grow... Let's grow.

I acknowledge my unique self

I acknowledge my authentic truth

I acknowledge my existence in this vast universe

I acknowledge my strength, I am resilient

I acknowledge that I am worthy, invaluable and irreplaceable

I acknowledge my unwavering determination to evolve and flourish

I acknowledge my vulnerabilities, viewing them as steppingstones towards personal growth

I acknowledge my dreams and craft pathways to make them a reality

I acknowledge that I will encounter moments of disappointment. I meet these moments with kindness and gentleness, understanding they are a part of my journey

I acknowledge that my peace is a choice I make

I acknowledge my feelings and choose to navigate my life with wisdom

I acknowledge my setbacks and actively seek ways to overcome them

I acknowledge my fears, recognizing them as mere
shadows in the brilliance of my courage

2

Dream

Dreaming is akin to envisioning.It is giving life to that which has no substance. Without vision, there can be no change, only chance. You see, change is for those with vision. If you desire to see a change, you must endeavor to dream and create an alternate reality other than the one you are currently taking part in.

Dreaming requires you to hope and believe with your heart that goodness will come through your endeavors towards your goals.

Dreaming requires you to close your eyes to what may be your circumstances and focus solely on what you envision. You must block out what will inhibit you from reaching your goal and focus on making strides towards your new reality.

I Dream as if no one is watching

I heed the calls of my heart

I am determined to fulfill my dreams

I always honor the commitments I make to myself

I create plans and diligently execute them

I intentionally curate my life

I discover my purpose

I allow myself to grieve if needed, but I choose to keep moving forward

I rewrite my story with empowering narratives

I relentlessly pursue my goals

I take deliberate steps towards my desires

I acknowledge that fear holds no power over my true potential

I am the master of my own life

I embrace the flow of my desires

I believe in my abilities, and so I take action

I can achieve anything I set my mind to

Victory is my destiny, as I refuse to accept defeat

Victory manifests through my intentional actions

I uncover success along my journey

My purpose fuels my diligent work

I am deserving of what I desire

I maintain hope

I dream big

I create strategic plans

I achieve my goals

I continually progress

I inspire others through my actions

I live a life of triumph

I never give up on myself

I refine my vision by adjusting my focus when necessary

I accomplish what I set out to do

I have unwavering faith

I believe in myself

3

Give

To give is an act of the heart, a selfless sharing from within without expecting anything in return. While giving often materializes in tangible forms, it also manifests in intangible gestures that are invisible to the naked eye.

It is the love you extend to someone, the kindness, empathy, understanding, truth, honor, a listening ear, and much more.

When one gives, it is akin to offering a piece of their essence to another being.

Giving holds the power to transform and imbue essence, fostering connection and energy. It is a profound act of creation.

I am captivated by the idea that through giving, energy is actualized, capable of inspiring and reshaping the environment around us.

Giving calls for us to forge connections with others, to be fully present, and to unleash the greatness within us to inspire love in the lives of those around us.

I give the gift of forgiveness

I grant gentleness to myself and those around me

I present the gift of kindness throughout my life experiences

I give the gift of truth

I endow myself with the gift of sovereignty over my journey

I give myself the gift of self acceptance

4

Expect

Disappointment arises when you rely on other people's plans for your life.It occurs when you move according to others' timing instead of taking initiative on your own. Disappointment arises when you cling to codependency instead of embracing the independence you were meant to have.

We were all created to exist independently, with a natural desire to connect. This connection should not hinder our independent nature but rather enhance it.

Disappointment arises when you believe that you need someone else to continue your journey of life independently.

Connection is undoubtedly one of the most delightful experiences one can have in life. However, it can become overwhelming when burdened by expectations, the need to please others, and the loss of one's own identity in order to fulfill someone else's desires.

Disappointment arises when we haven't learned to rely on ourselves and instead seek support from others to stand on our own two feet. Unfortunately, this reliance never truly makes standing easier because we constantly lean on others, neglecting to develop the strength and resilience to navigate life independently.

Ultimately, disappointment arises from our refusal to fully embrace and live our own lives to the fullest.

It's important to recognize that disappointment is not caused by external factors; rather, it is an internal experience that manifests as a result of our own choices.

I expect

I expect a beautiful life

I expect peace

I expect good things to happen to me

I expect moments of serendipity

I expect growth

I expect change

5

Grow

Parents love their young and will go to great lengths to protect them. However, even in their love, there comes a point where they must let go and allow their children to grow beyond what is within their limited perspective.

There is a vast world out there, filled with possibilities and opportunities that may differ from what others envision for you. It is important to ask yourself: What is your own vision?

Have you become so caught up in the expectations and visions others have for your life that you have neglected to explore and embrace the greatness that lies before you? It's time to break free from those constraints and allow yourself to wonder, to explore, and to discover the unique path that awaits you.

I understand that comfort hinders growth

I choose to flourish

I recognize that my growth is dependent on persistent progress, which will gradually transform into a fulfilling journey of self improvement

Growth occurs when I embrace discomfort

I stretch

                        I strive

I rest, observe, and reset with a fresh perspective

I overcome all resistance encountered during my growth

I combat stagnation through action

My growth is independent of the comfort levels of those around me

I embrace growth in all life's seasons

My growth necessitates effort, and so I put in the work

I refuse to settle

My energy is precious

My time is valuable

6

Shift

What if you discovered a purpose to live for? What if, by letting go, you unearthed the very essence of your existence? The rhythm that sets your life in motion, the lyrics that harmonize with the melody you've been quietly humming. What if the answer to your long-standing question has always been within reach, but the complexities of your mind obscured it from view?

You were destined for greatness, placed into existence by divine design, shattering the mold as you emerged. Your very presence emanates vibrations of boundless potential and endless possibilities, yet your story remains untold, stifled by the hidden reservoirs of your untapped capabilities.

What if your destiny was greatness, but your vision became clouded and everything seemed to indicate that it was too late? What if time, instead of working against you, actually worked in your favor, allowing a single second to stretch into an eternity, even as life continued to move forward? In this scenario, time would cease to be a limiting factor, and an abundance of minutes, hours, and days would be at your disposal to fulfill every dream and aspiration you could possibly imagine.

Now, imagine if this were the case. Would a shift begin to occur? The very movement created by the endless possibilities and "what if's" would reside within the shifting nature of time. No moment would ever slip away again, and the present moment would be all that we have. This would disrupt the very fabric of what society dictates as the norm, and we would enter a realm of shifting possibilities. What if, indeed, a shift began to happen?

My transformation is continuous

Shifting reminds me of my strength

Shifting fortifies my resilience

Shifting urges me to be present within myself

I transform

I dare to venture

I adapt

I make new choices

I alter my responses

I discover routes to harmonious living

The realization of my potential ignites my freedom

7

Manifest

What does it truly take for something to become visible, tangible, and present? I have dedicated considerable time pondering the process of bringing forth something into existence. Through my reflections, I have come to realize that it requires effort, care, and pride. Often, transforming an idea into a physical reality demands a significant amount of energy.

To achieve this, we must be willing to invest our time, resources, and energy. I understand that along the journey, weariness may set in, and it is during these moments that we are most prone to giving up. When gratification seems delayed, hope can waver, and we may convince ourselves that our efforts will never come to fruition.

During the process of manifestation, it is crucial to nurture our vision. This entails dedicating time and effort to ensure that the idea we have conceived does not wither away. It means safeguarding our idea, conducting research, cultivating it, trying new approaches, and making necessary adjustments to reach our ultimate goal. Our idea becomes something tangible, visible, and present.

It is when we take pride in our vision, investing great care and effort to prevent it from fading away, that we begin to manifest remarkable things. The journey will not be easy; it will be a battle of the mind. I want you to recognize that you possess more strength than you realize! There will be moments when you feel like giving up and surrendering. Even in those challenging times, you have the resilience to persevere! Do not succumb to the false narratives that sometimes plague your mind. You are capable of achieving all that you hope for. Be persistent, give your best effort, and take immense pride in and care of what you are doing.

My actions align with what I want to manifest

Faith is the manifestation of work

My substance can only manifest through my work

I take action to manifest my hopes

I expect my wildest dreams to manifest

My consistent work will manifest my hopes

I have the ability to manifest great things

Growth is painful, but beautiful when it manifests

I manifest

I cultivate

Harmony manifest peace in my life

I plan, then manifest

8

Be present

The question that has been occupying my thoughts is: What do I truly need in this moment? While I haven't fully unraveled the answer, a few immediate desires surface within my heart: love, connection, authenticity, and presence. Above all, I yearn for a sense of presence.

I long to be truly seen, deeply felt, genuinely heard, and profoundly understood. I crave the feeling of being desired and accepted by those around me.

Gone are the days of fussing, fighting, and embracing misery. I no longer wish to engage in such negativity.

I often find myself contemplating my own presence and the inevitable reality that one day I will be gone. It frustrates me when I allow my thoughts to dwell in that space, yet I find myself returning to it all too frequently.

Questions flood my mind: "Why does this even matter? Why must we all face death?" Sometimes, I surrender before even attempting to find answers. The concept of death can bring about unrest and a reluctance to fight.

But what do you do when faced with a reality that is both expected and unchangeable?

You accept it.

You merge with it.

You live it.

You make a conscious choice to engage and be fully present.

Instead of allowing the fear or uncertainty of death to consume you, you embrace it as an integral part of life. By accepting its inevitability, you can find a deeper appreciation for the present moment and make the most of the time you have.

I occupy

I take up space

I create space for myself

I exist

I show up

I show up with a spirit of excellence

I rest knowing that I am enough

I will simply be great

I communicate concisely and effectively

I choose to radiate positivity and goodness

9

Realize

Dear Mr. Righting My Wrongs,

I must acknowledge the ways in which I have wronged you, driven by misguided reasons. I have eagerly embraced opportunities that appeared to be right, only to discover that they were, in fact, entirely wrong.

I have rushed to conclusions about your intentions, failing to recognize the clear evidence that was right before my eyes. I have lived under the haze of your presence, losing sight of what was supposedly right in front of me. It pains me to admit that I simply could not see.

But now, I am actively rectifying my mistakes. I am embracing the power of my own vision. It is disheartening to realize that it took all of this to truly see the corruption within you, and in that corruption, I lost a part of myself.

Yet, here I stand with newfound courage! I am reclaiming my strength and reclaiming my voice that was once silenced. I am demolishing the walls that were once fortified with lies and constructed by the hands of deceivers.

My mere presence has the ability to shatter bonds. My strength is sufficient to make the right choices. I am more than enough in my own existence. I am enough.

So, dear Mr., I am actively making amends for my past wrongs.

I am aware and open

I realize my potential is often hidden in plain sight

I realize that I am one-of-a-kind

I realize that my life is blessed and that I am a blessing

I realize that potential is embodied by me

I open my eyes to see that I am valuable, this allows me to experience the greatness of my being

10

Choose

How many of you find yourselves caught in the trap of dwelling?

This tendency may manifest as overthinking, endlessly discussing a topic without making any progress, or feeling stuck in a particular area of your life. Dwelling can take various forms and shapes, but at its core, it signifies a lack of forward motion – remaining stagnant without any change.

You might wonder why dwelling is not acceptable. The answer lies in the fact that there is no growth in stagnancy. Being stagnant holds you back and drains the vitality out of your life. It hinders your ability to achieve your goals and aspirations.

Stagnancy can be defined as a state of inactivity, where things are not flowing or progressing. It signifies a lack of development, advancement, or forward movement.

When we consciously choose to dwell, we are essentially choosing to remain stagnant. We make a decision to not progress beyond a certain point, as if we are placing a self-imposed cap on our own growth.

Now, let me clarify that I have personally engaged in dwelling throughout my life. However, I have come to realize that at some point, a decision must be made, and action must follow that decision. I had a moment of self-reflection where I thought to myself, "Did you know that overthinking can actually hold you back?"

This refers to the act of continuously mulling over an idea in our minds, going in circles without taking any tangible action based on those thoughts. It is a form of dwelling where we get trapped in our own thoughts without translating them into meaningful actions.

How can we free ourselves from this pattern of activity? The answer lies in taking a leap into the unknown. Often, what keeps us stuck is our fear of the unknown. We are afraid of the potential outcomes if we take certain actions, and we play out various scenarios in our minds. As a result, time passes by, and yet, nothing changes.

However, it is important to note that there is a place for reflection and contemplation, which I refer to as observation. This involves intentionally setting aside a specific amount of time to think things through and assess what is going well or not so well in our current situation. After this period of observation, taking action becomes crucial.

During this phase, we make decisions about whether to continue with what has been working for us, making necessary adjustments, or removing obstacles that hinder our progress. We may also choose to readjust something that has shown some success but could potentially be improved upon.

By combining thoughtful observation with decisive action, we can break free from the cycle of dwelling and move towards positive change and growth.

It is my choice to make good and produce with the skills I have been given

I choose love, this means choosing to speak the truth with respect and integrity

Instead of choosing to be at war with myself, I choose peace

I choose to be happy

Happiness is my choice

I make the best choices for me

My choices manifest my outcome

Nothing is off-limits everything is a choice

I choose freedom

I choose love

I choose me

I choose wisely

My peace is my choice

I honor my choices

My fulfillment is grown through my choice to be happy

I will not feel guilty for choosing what is best for me

When I find myself in the middle of a mental battle, I choose not to surrender

At times when I feel exhausted while doing the necessary work, I remember the reason for my journey and choose to progress forward

I intentionally cultivate joy by choosing what will cause my joy to bloom

I am in full bloom when I choose my joy

My Joy is my choice

I am a winner by choice

I choose to be victorious

I am not defined by moments but instead by the journey I
choose to live

I choose not to disappoint myself

I choose to be honest with myself so that I can grow

When I choose peace I attract clarity in my life

I grow because I choose not to turn away from what is hard

My growth is my choice

I choose what I want for my life

I choose to do all that I want to with my life

When I am confident in myself I make better decisions

I accept only what I am worthy of

I trust

I encounter

I arrive

I decide what I want, and I move towards it

I Simply decide

I decide to do the hard work

I decide nothing will stop me

I decide to be true to myself

I decide to be persistent

I decide to hold onto my power

I decide to execute my power

I decide to live my truth

I decide to embody my own greatness

I decide to be different

I decide to bring change

I decide to outgrow stagnancy

I make decisions

When I make decisions it is always based on the life I want to lead

11

Honor

Honor encompasses reverence and respect towards something or someone. In moments of meditation, I am deeply moved as I ponder the vastness of life. Upon awakening, I realize my ability to move, to exist, to think—I am alive. I acknowledge that I am present in an existence beyond my comprehension, a gift undeserved.

Contemplating how to live purposefully, I strive to be fully present, honoring the precious gift of life bestowed upon me. I recognize that being mindful of the abundance of blessings around me is a way to honor existence.

To honor is to recognize a truth and deliberately create space to show reverence for that truth.

Acknowledgment is essential for honor to manifest.

I honor God, the author and finisher of my life

I honor journeying in this life

I honor who I have been created to be

I honor the time I have been given to fulfill my innate purpose

I honor every circumstance in my life, and navigate patiently through them

12

Allow

Allowance, in many ways, is connected to the concept of boundaries. To allow is to offer a certain amount of room and acceptance; it represents a positive affirmation rather than a declaration of an end.

Creating space for allowance fosters understanding. It facilitates growth and nourishes relationships as well as broadens mindsets.

In a sense, allowance serves as a form of open exploration. It conveys the message, "In this space, you are free to be."

Allowance implies granting permission to yourself, to a circumstance, or to another person to simply exist. Rather than inhibiting, it encourages the presence and existence of remarkable possibilities.

I allow my work to speak to my belief

I allow my intentions to be my reason

I will not allow my life to be consumed by tragedy, instead I choose joy

I never allow others to tell me who I am

I am allowed to be true to myself

I let go of excuses and allow myself fulfillment

Happiness grows when I allow it to

I allow myself to observe and engage with life

I allow life to teach me what to do next

I allow myself to engage with my fears, so that I overcome them

I allow myself to let go of what no longer serves me

I allow my light to shine

I allow myself to be free regardless of others

I allow joy to warm my heart

I allow myself to grow in all areas of my life

13

Purpose

As Jesus said, "If you bring forth what is within you, what you bring forth will save you. If you do not bring forth what is within you, what you do not bring forth will destroy you" (Thomas 70:3).

Does a fruit tree need guidance to bear fruit? Or is it naturally ingrained in its essence to produce the fruit it is meant to yield?

Yet, as humans, we often grapple with defining our purpose. We vacillate, hoping to arrive at a conclusion, often failing to appreciate the journey along the way.

What if our purpose was embedded deep within us, and all we truly needed to do was quiet our minds and unearth the blueprint already imprinted within our being? That is purpose.

Our purpose is our conscious decision to be authentically ourselves. A pear tree doesn't bear apples; nor does it gaze at an apple tree and yearn to yield apples. Instead, it instinctively knows it was designed to bear pears, and it joyfully produces what is in its inherent nature to yield.

Purpose poses the question, "What is within you?" If you are in alignment with your true self, your life will be purposeful. If you are out of alignment, you risk becoming like a tree that bears no fruit.

My purpose is my choice

Unfulfillment is the enemy of purpose, so I choose to be fulfilled

If I choose something that does not align with self, then I am outside of my purpose

My purpose causes me to be productive

If I want to feel purposeful, I must get moving

I allow my work to align with my purpose

I live life on purpose

I separate from what does not serve my purpose

Live! the purpose of life is to live

I am determined to accomplish what I intentionally set out to do

I greet each morning with my intentions for the day

I greet my day with fulfillment

I greet my day with a hopeful spirit

I take courage

14

Rest

There is an undeniable aspect of life that remains beyond our control, and that is death. While this notion may evoke feelings of solitude, the reality is that death is an integral part of our existence. In fact, it is through the very process of living that we are continuously moving closer to our ultimate "rest" – death.

Death serves as a significant reminder to make the most of our lives. It prompts us to actively engage in our existence rather than passively allowing life to unfold before us. By acknowledging the inevitability of death, we are encouraged to take an active role in shaping our lives and making the most of each moment.

Life truly begins when we discover inner peace and rest within ourselves. It is through the courage to pursue our aspirations and manifest beyond our initial circumstances that we unlock our true potential.

Many of us are born into limited environments, akin to a fish bowl, where our knowledge and experiences are confined by glass walls. However, beyond the boundaries of this fish bowl lie vast oceans, rivers, and lakes waiting to be explored.

At times, fear becomes a barrier that prevents us from venturing outside the fishbowl. This fear may be perpetuated by the voices of others who are also confined within the fishbowl or even by individuals who have managed to escape but wish to see us remain stagnant.

Nevertheless, it is crucial to overcome these fears and break free from the limitations of the fish bowl. By doing so, we can embark on a journey of exploration, growth, and fulfillment, discovering the vastness of possibilities that lie beyond our initial confinement.

Finding peace within oneself is essential to truly start living. In order to achieve peace with the ultimate rest, one must first find peace with their ultimate life.

The key to finding inner peace lies in actively living one's life. By embracing and fully experiencing the journey, we can cultivate a sense of harmony within ourselves. It is through living authentically and aligning our actions with our values that we can attain a state of tranquility and contentment.

Rather than passively existing, it is by actively engaging in life that we can discover the peace that resides within us. By embracing our true selves and living in accordance with our passions and purpose, we can embark on a path towards inner peace and a fulfilling life.

I am never disappointed with myself because I am content with who I am

My desire to connect never stifles who I am

I have the strength to stand on my own

I embrace the expectations I set for myself, and let go of the expectations others have for me

I embrace my life and live it to its fullest

I invest in myself

I acknowledge my needs, and I give myself what I need

I am present, I am alive

I am intentional with how I spend my time and energy

I greet this moment acknowledging the greatness of my being

It's ok, I'm okay, and I'm doing the best that can

15

Identity

Do we know who we are? At the core of our being, who are we? Made up of unique gene coding and personality traits these things come together to form our being.

It's interesting that many of us never actually take the time to get to know ourselves the way that we would take the time to get to know others. So busy with pleasing and engaging the world around us we neglect self.

Do we consciously know what makes us happy? Do we know what makes us tick? Do we truly know what we enjoy and why?

There is something to be said about finding rest in self... but true rest can only happen when we have taken the hard journey to discover who we are.

Along the way I have learned that others sometimes influence our thoughts about self.. but honestly, the truth is we are only influenced when we don't understand our own truth. We are moved and become unsteady because we have not taken the time to ground ourselves and grow roots in our identity.

Identity is not made up of fictional thoughts, instead it is grounded in facts. What are our facts? Is it what the world has to "declare" or is it what we declare?

We declare by our words, we declare by our actions, we declare by our being.

We declare our identity

I inspire

I answer my tough internal questions

No one has the answer to who I am but me

I live an extraordinary life

When I connect with myself, I discover my self worth

I don't hide in the shadows

I never change who I am to fit their mold

I respect myself

I teach others how to treat me by showing them

I stop trying to be perfect

I understand that I am human

I vibe with myself

I show up authentically

I embrace the strength in my weaknesses

I curse the feelings of worthlessness

I renounce lies of self deception

I embrace the beauty in my being

I find myself completely immersed in who I am

I expect greatness from myself

I empathize, but I don't betray myself

I reconcile my feelings with self

I comfort myself

I attend to my own needs

I hold a deep reverence for my own being

I show up and I am present

I speak my truth

I will not be afraid to use my voice

I always stand in my truth

I will always be excited for myself

I embrace every moment of my life with positivity, leaving no room for regrets

I embrace and celebrate all aspects of who I am

I embrace my differences

I deserve goodness

I live authentically

I effortlessly attract meaningful connections, and align with individuals who resonate with my authentic self

I trust myself

I liberate myself from the shackles of self-deprecating thoughts and embrace a mindset of positivity and self-empowerment

I am confident in my inner wisdom and trust that I will always choose what is truly best for myself

I am the ultimate authority in choosing what is best for me

I now stride fearlessly, embracing triumph in every step I take

I embrace and cherish every moment of my existence

Each breath that I take gives me the courage to keep going

My presence is enough

I walk in my light

I prioritize the cultivation of inner peace and actively seek harmony in all aspects of my existence

16

I am

I have been struggling with thoughts of self hatred; The thoughts of not being enough, not knowing how to make the right decisions for me. Trying really hard to make things work in a way that might make me feel better, but at the root of everything,

"I hate myself."

I see the ugliness in me, the wanting to be loved, the wanting to be accepted, the wanting to be good enough. But the truth is

"I don't feel like I'm good enough."

I have been pointing my vision outwards to find validation from the world around me. However, I have to figure out how to value me for who I am at any given season in my life.

I hate myself, and no matter what you think love and hate cannot abide in the same space.

If I desire to walk in my light then the flame of hate must be put out and replaced with a roaring fire of love that cannot only consume but a roaring fire that can never be outed.

My passion for self must roar so greatly that all you see is the luminant light that captivates all who beholds its beauty!

Understanding that my flame may not suit everyone, but for those who can withstand its greatness, and interact without being burnt, welcome.

I am present with myself

I am bold When I decide to share who I am

I am a miracle

If I am looking for answers I will find in love

I am complete in love

I am consistent

I am strong

I am persistent

I am enough

I am worthy

I am the embodiment of potential

I am resilient

I am bold

I am calm

I am fearless and courageous

I am open

I am making the best choices for me

I am present

I am gentle

I am loving on me

I am not afraid of failure because it is life's way of telling me to try another way

I am in harmony with myself, and peace surrounds me

I am aware of self

I am blessed, and I am a blessing

17

Peace

Peace begins within.

It requires making peace with oneself, which entails ending the internal battles that constantly rage in your mind. It's about raising the white flag and accepting yourself for who you truly are.

The struggle often lies in acknowledging your true self. It's like a tug of war; one moment you're here, the next you're there. You may find yourself questioning why this internal conflict exists in the first place. This war arises because your alignment with your true self is skewed.

Often, we look outwardly, using the actions of the majority as a moral compass. However, this approach can lead us to align ourselves with the world rather than with our true selves. True peace can only be achieved when we are in harmony with our thoughts, feelings, and inner world.

Peace is about self-control, and self-control stems from self-knowledge. Once you truly know yourself, you can provide what you need. However, without self-knowledge, self-control becomes virtually impossible, and without self-control, peace remains elusive.

Take some time to be still, close your eyes, and drown out the surrounding noise. Find your inner voice and listen to what it's telling you. This is the path to finding peace.

My life is too precious to live it in anger

I rest

I rest in hope

I renew my mind daily

I feel my feelings

I embrace the sunshine

I tame my thoughts

I don't turn away from the things that scare me

I home in on my voice

I block out the noise

I take time to be still

I practice gratitude

I slow down

I find my flow

I Meditate

I take time for myself

                                I stand

I take time to go for walks

I take time to watch the sunset

I get lost in a good book

I laugh

I spend time with friends

I spend time with family

I take control of my time

I share moments of joy with those around me

I forgive

I greet each moment with the decision to be good to myself

I find peace in taking good care of myself

I am at peace when I decide for myself

I am the master of my life

In my peace I am one with myself

I make decisions that support my peace

18

Love

I had to make the choice to embrace love during a time when I felt disturbed by the negativity surrounding me.

It was a challenging experience to be judged and put on trial by those I held close to my heart. I felt a whirlwind of emotions knowing the truth, yet not being given the opportunity to defend myself. What do you do when you're dealt cards you don't even know how to play?

I confronted each person involved, expressing my disappointment in their negative actions. However, I found myself unsatisfied by their lack of remorse and their excuses attempting to justify their behavior. They smeared my name with lies, defamed my character, and played a role in the enemy's scheme to attack me. It's ironic how the concept of "character" comes into play here.

In this moment, as I strive to live my life with the utmost integrity, God has been speaking to me about the importance of integrity. It means doing what's right even when no one is watching. I believe I am a woman of integrity, so it deeply hurt me to discover that people I cherished had been tarnishing my integrity.

I was faced with a choice: whether to allow these individuals to push me towards unforgiveness and hatred or to rise above it. Ignoring the elephant in the room is not always easy. I had to speak my truth and put an end to the lies they were spreading about me.

Throughout it all, I had to approach the situation with respect and love. Choosing love doesn't mean accepting the negativity that others throw at you. Choosing love means speaking the truth with integrity and respect. It means refusing to let others break or defeat you. It means declaring your truth while standing against the lies people try to spread about you.

Choosing love can manifest in various ways. Ultimately, it is a decision that not only enhances your own life and character but also positively impacts those around you.

I embrace the gift of love within myself

My love uplifts and inspires

I both give and receive love abundantly

I value and appreciate my own efforts

I walk through life with love as my guide

I am aware of the presence of love within me

I prioritize self-care and nurture myself with love

I start each day by greeting it with love

My love is expansive, unrestricted, and built on trust

I hold love in high regard and honor its power

Love reciprocates and respects my choices

Love is a conscious decision I make

Love overcomes fear; choosing love is choosing freedom

Love is a precious gift I cherish

Love embraces and encompasses all aspects of life

19

Joy

I find joy in unexpected places. When I am not looking for it, it appears. It finds me wherever I am and often taken by its peace and desire to warm my heart and brighten my smile.

Joy remedies the overbearing feelings of stress… joy comforts me in times of mourning, joy brings song to my heart and a rhythmic bop to my head.

Joy overwhelms me with life's beauty and blesses me with the desire to carry on

In times of desperation my heart cries to joy! It yells for her to come engulf me with her peace. At times no matter what I do, I cannot find joy…

But there is something special about joy's presence… she shows up at the most unexpected times, in the most unexpected ways… when she is present… man she is present. And my heart rejoices In her being…

See, I know what it means to be sad… I know what it means to be hopeless…I know what it means to not want to carry on.

But joy! Today, my heart, though heavy with disappointment...
It is remedied by unexpected moments of joy.

I find joy in unexpected places.

I do what I enjoy

I acknowledge my joy

I enjoy life's beauty

I expect joy

I greet my day with the spirit of joy

I am worthy of joy

I find joy in my day-to-day living

I welcome joy every day

Joy never escapes me

My joy inspires my gratitude and points out the goodness in my life

I am inspired by joy

Joy is never fleeting because each moment presents another opportunity to be engulfed by her

My joy is worthy

I Celebrate

I celebrate my wins

Joy blesses me with her presence every day

I find joy in unexpected places

Joy finds me wherever I am

My heart is remedied by joys intrinsic presence

I intentionally create moments of joy in my life

20

Happiness

Why is happiness often seen as the ultimate prize, as if it is the pinnacle of all rewards?

I have come to realize that happiness is not a destination but a continuous choice to follow the truth in your heart. It involves walking in faith towards the life and purpose woven into your being.

Happiness is an inner journey, not an external pursuit. When you genuinely connect with your spirit and have the courage to act upon its guidance, happiness naturally emerges as a byproduct.

The true treasures lie in self-realization, courage, and embracing an authentic existence.

When you live authentically, happiness radiates into all aspects of your life.

Happiness blooms from knowing myself

My happiness is contingent upon no one but me

Happiness remains when I consistently prioritize my well-being by honoring and nurturing myself

There is an abundance of happiness around me

I walk out my life daily in love and happiness

I live

I greet my day with gratitude

I cultivate love, joy, peace, patience, kindness, goodness, faithfulness, gentleness, and self-control

Happiness is a conscious decision and an ongoing practice of nurturing my mind. It entails actively choosing to engage in mental exercises that promote joy and well-being

21

Action

Starting can often be the most difficult part of any endeavor.

The task before you may seem like an insurmountable obstacle, making the mere idea of beginning feel nearly impossible. Doubt wages an internal war, making you question whether you are truly capable of reaching your goal.

I have found myself more often than not on the brink of greatness, only to be halted by an onslaught of self-sabotage. Self-sabotage prevents you from progressing towards the goals that resonate within your heart and mind.

In one past experience, my emotions ran high and I felt paralyzed, incapable of advancing towards what I needed to accomplish. However, it was a task that simply needed completion. Pushing past my feelings was essential. Once I started and accomplished what felt like a mountainous task, I learned a crucial lesson. Often, it's not the obstacle that's impossible, but rather the apprehension that precedes it.

Faith encourages us to see with our eyes, but feel with our hearts the greatness achievable through persistence and endurance. It calls us to action. Faith without action is hollow, whereas faith followed by targeted action brings to life the visions conceived in our hearts.

I choose to keep moving forward because my well-being depends on it

My actions catalyze change

My progress is contingent upon my actions

Without movement, my desired change will remain elusive

My actions affirm my worthiness

With a clear vision, direction follows naturally

I am accountable for manifesting my desires

My empowerment fuels action

I am capable and competent

I am able to accomplish anything

My strength, derived from my creator, enables me to do all things

Printed in the USA
CPSIA information can be obtained
at www.ICGtesting.com
LVHW020820210724
786028LV00010B/193